IT SHOULDN'T HAPPEN
(TO A DOG)

It Shouldn't Happen (To a Dog)

Don Freeman

FOREWORD BY
TODD DePASTINO

DOVER PUBLICATIONS, INC.
MINEOLA, NEW YORK

The Publisher would like to thank Roy Freeman
for the use of the illustrations in the Foreword.

Copyright

Foreword to the Dover Edition Copyright © 2014
by Todd DePastino
All rights reserved.

Bibliographical Note

It Shouldn't Happen (to a Dog) is an unabridged republication of *It Shouldn't Happen—*, originally published in 1945 by Harcourt, Brace and Company, New York. Todd DePastino has supplied a new Foreword to this edition.

Library of Congress Cataloging-in-Publication Data

Freeman, Don, 1908-1978.
   [It shouldn't happen]
   It shouldn't happen (to a dog) / Don Freeman ; foreword by Todd DePastino.
      pages cm
   Summary: "Recounted chiefly in winsome illustrations, this fantasy of a GI who's transformed into a dog offers a witty take on WWII-era life among soldiers and on the home front. "Wonderful fun." — Chicago Tribune"— Provided by publisher.
   ISBN-13: 978-0-486-78210-2 (paperback)
   ISBN-10: 0-486-78210-7
   1. American wit and humor, Pictorial. 2. United States. Army—Military life—History—20th century—Pictorial works. I. DePastino, Todd, writer of supplementary textual content. II. Title.

NC1429.F6677A4 2014
741.5'6973—dc23

                           2014018925

Manufactured in the United States by Courier Corporation
78210701   2014
www.doverpublications.com

Foreword to the Dover Edition

At a glance, this first publication since 1945 of Don Freeman's *It Shouldn't Happen*—a book the cartoonist Seth has called an important "signpost on the way to the 'graphic novel'"—might seem of interest only to antiquarians or aficionados of comics history. But this book about the adventures of a young man drafted into the army and turned into a dog is, in fact, a masterwork of satiric allegory that championed the cause of racial equality, sparked controversy when first published, and still resonates today.

It's a tribute indeed to the democratic principles with which the United States fought World War II that they were liberal enough to permit Don Freeman, himself a soldier, to publish this book during wartime. America's enemies didn't allow such sharp social critiques, no matter how tempered, as this book is, by tenderness, humor, and a good-natured faith in ordinary citizens. Of course, if all readers were like the reviewer who declared "there is nothing serious about *It Shouldn't Happen* . . . [it] is pure fantasy," then Don Freeman wouldn't have had to fret about stirring trouble. More worrisome was the hysterical New York Times review of August 26, 1945, which contended that *It Shouldn't Happen* was "race propaganda . . . calculated to encourage bitterness and hatred . . . [and] to suggest that justice is best achieved by violence." This reviewer, at least, got the point of the book, even if he grossly distorted it for a reactionary purpose.

This harsh reception of *It Shouldn't Happen*—coming within days of Japan's surrender—marked the reigniting of a culture war first kindled in the Great Depression and dampened by Pearl Harbor. The war years were a time out of time for America, when life plans—and culture wars—were put on hold. Finishing school, advancing a career, even buying a new car or stove all had to wait, and that included the aspirations of workers, ethnics, and African Americans. These groups had struggled during the 1930s for union recognition, Civil Rights, and New Deal social protections. Bolstering this movement was a broad upsurge in the popular arts that scholar Michael

Foreword to the Dover Edition

Denning has called the "cultural front," a "second American Renaissance" involving artists, musicians, and writers ranging from Woody Guthrie and Duke Ellington to Orson Welles and cartoonists laboring in Disney's studios. The war effort muted the insurgency, as everyone fell in line to support the "Arsenal of Democracy" in its global war against fascism. When that war ended in the summer of 1945—the time Don Freeman's cartoon satire was released—the cultural front was poised for a breakthrough. Victory in Europe and the Pacific had rid the world of Hitler, Mussolini, and Tojo. Now was the time, many liberals and leftists believed, for Jim Crow to join them in the dustbin of history.

Don Freeman had been a part of the cultural front from the very beginning, when at the age of twenty-one he hitchhiked cross country to New York City, arriving days before the stock market crash of 1929. He came to New York as a dance band musician, playing trumpet in nightclubs and at wedding receptions, while taking classes at the famous Art Students League with Ash Can School founder John Sloan. Sloan was one of the first modern realist painters to use his brush to further the causes of Socialism and social justice. Sloan encouraged Don to do what he loved: wander the bustling streets and sketch them in all their bewildering diversity. He went everywhere and sketched everyone, especially the marginal and down-and-out, whom he captured often with humor and always compassion. Don's boyhood fondness for the theater blossomed in New York, where he attended plays as often as he could, sketchbook in hand. Don's New York sketches quickly numbered into the thousands. His only worry, he said later, was that the store would run out of drawing paper.

A turn in career happened late one night as he was returning from an Italian wedding reception. Busily sketching the subway scene, he stepped off the train at Sheridan Square before realizing he'd left his trumpet behind. He swung round as the doors closed and watched his horn, still on his seat, disappear into the darkness. His response to the lost moneymaker was characteristic of the resilient and entrepreneurial Don. He took a bundle of his Broadway sketches to the offices of the New York *Herald-Tribune's* drama department. They began publishing his work, and Don became a professional artist.

Foreword to the Dover Edition

Graphic artists and painters then and now must master many skills to survive, and, in addition to selling his theater drawings to magazines and newspapers, Don turned to printmaking and lithography. For a while, he made posters for the New Deal WPA's Federal Arts Project. Then, he turned to book illustrations, providing, for example, the pictures to William Saroyan's words in *The Human Comedy*. He even self-published his own his subscription magazine, *Don Freeman's Newsstand, One Man's View of Manhattan*, or, *"All the News that Fits to Prints."* Selling initially at fifty cents a copy, the *Newsstand* bristled with color and energy, chronicling through drawings and Don's commentary the life of the city. As art historian Michelle Gabriel put it, "No other artist has been credited with recording so faithfully and with such sensitivity the drama of New York City as Don Freeman." Other artists called him the "Daumier of New York," in reference to the legendary French caricaturist, whose drawings captured and satirized nineteenth-century Parisian society, eventually landing him in jail.

Don Freeman almost suffered a similar fate, but not because of his drawings. In the summer of 1943, Don received his draft notice. Any observer could have predicted that a thirty-five-year-old left-wing artist would not likely find the army a comfortable fit. It's safe to say that most of the other 10 million American men drafted into service weren't happy either. Ordinary Americans walking around free one day suddenly found themselves regimented by military autocrats and subordinated at the bottom of a very tall hierarchy. Famed combat cartoonist and infantry sergeant Bill Mauldin called the army a "caste system" where officers were nobility and enlisted men "peasants." "The caste system makes it a degrading and humiliating thing to be an enlisted man, and it shouldn't be," he said. New inductees faced a training regimen designed, it seemed, to debase the soldier's humanity to something lesser, such as a dog or a tool.

The enlisted man's only defense was humor, and army vernacular is so replete with inside jokes they're hardly even noticed. Identification necklaces became *"dog tags"*; a one-person shelter was a *"pup-tent"*; defensive fighting positions were called *"foxholes"*; and combat infantrymen themselves became *"dogfaces."* Even the common term

"G.I." was born in sardonic self-reference to "government issue," a soldier reduced to a piece of equipment, like an "M1943 Entrenching Tool" or "Shoes, Service, Composition, Sole (Type II)." When Don Freeman's Pvt. Albert C. Bedlington, Jr., literally turns into a dog, he's just following the process begun in basic training to its logical extreme.

So, it's no surprise that Don would have run into problems in the army. What's shocking is that he liked it as much as he did, a testament to what his son Roy describes as his father's perpetually upbeat and optimistic attitude. The army also made it easy on Don by assigning him an MOS (military occupational specialty) that actually fit his civilian profile. Don worked in Headquarters Company of the 42nd Infantry "Rainbow" Division at Camp Gruber, Oklahoma, reporting and illustrating for the *Rainbow Reveille* and *Gruber Guidon*. The job sent him all over the 30,000-man facility sketching camp life, just as

he had done on the streets of New York. He wrote home to his wife Lydia after a day on maneuvers: "It was really thrilling to go around thru the trees in the twilight and run into fellas I know . . . almost indistinguishable midst the leaves . . . perfect deception . . .The sky was particularly wonderful tonight . . . and the way the guys stood up against it . . . and to go to sleep on the ground while there's always a guard watching over . . . no lights anywhere . . . this is real tactical stuff."

It didn't take long, however, for Don's attitude to sour as he fell afoul of a segregated army that was quick to punish those who challenged its racial conventions. Just how Don's troubles began isn't entirely clear. Don's letters to Lydia describe in elliptical prose an incident at a "shindig" held at the camp's Officers' Club in 1944. Division commander Maj. Gen. Harry J. Collins presided over the party, which got a little rowdy on account of smuggled liquor (Oklahoma was a dry state in the 1940s). Don, merely a private, was there sketching caricatures and also, perhaps, playing trumpet with the band. With him were three African American enlisted men, probably members of the all-black 333rd Field Artillery Battalion stationed in a strictly segregated section of camp.* "Every once in a while," Don recounts to Lydia, "certain unruly officers" shot "hot words and looks" at Don's black friends. "You can imagine what the remarks were—race prejudice blurted out." Don and his friends tried to ignore the offenses, and Don even penned a portrait for the general, but he could barely contain his fury. "I was a smoldering guy," he writes. "You can't know, of course, what a position it is to be in—privates midst these rankers! . . . It was tough—us 4 boys sweated blood and we couldn't wait to leave the place. . . . We were wrecks from the experience . . . I was plenty burned up."

Burned up enough to tell others about the racial harassment his low-ranking buddies had endured at the party. Don was disciplined for insubordination, and he apparently protested, arguing that the drunken lieutenants were the ones who should be punished, especially

---

*Eleven members of this battalion were later captured, tortured and executed by a German SS unit in the Belgian village of Wereth during the Battle of the Bulge.

given the ban on liquor. The case escalated, perhaps joined with other "offenses" Don may have committed, into a possible court-martial trial. Don was eventually saved by a brand new provision just added to the Military Justice Procedure handbook precisely to deal with delicate situations like this one. Army Regulation 615-369 allowed for an honorable administrative discharge being granted to an "undesirable" enlisted man who "may not only get into trouble himself but may corrupt others." Such a soldier, the provision explained, "should be eliminated before his continued presence causes disciplinary problems" in the unit. With that, Don traveled in November to Fort Dix, New Jersey, where he officially returned to civilian life.

Before mustering out, Don conspired with a friend on the *Rainbow Reveille,* Corporal Tom D. Murray, to write a book that would touch upon the controversy. "You'd get a kick outa what Tom and I are up to," he told Lydia. "It's a short book idea that I'm pretty darn certain will be the book I can have Harcourt take . . . the title *It Shouldn't Happen* . . . a story in pictures of a character to be known as Albert C. Harrington Jr. It was bound to come to this . . . they take everything or anything now, and so Al being a dog had something to offer in the service . . . he was drafted that's all there is to it . . . except he's bunked up with us and took his training like a man." It appears that, in Don and Tom's original idea, the protagonist is a dog from the beginning, mistakenly conscripted into the Army . . . and no one notices the error.

After Don's discharge, Tom Murray handed his interest in the project over to Don, who then took the fable concept in a new direction. The protagonist, now "Bedlington," turns into a dog in basic training. What could then become a scathing satire of the army broadens into a sharp critique of the civilian world. Indeed, Bedlington at first encounters no trouble whatsoever in camp. His fellow GIs either don't notice or don't care he's a dog. After all, they're virtually dogs themselves. It's only when he leaves on a three-day pass that he runs into problems. A bus driver orders him to sit with the African American soldiers in the back. Bedlington, years before Rosa Parks, refuses to give up his seat. The driver yells at him growling, "Where d'ya think y'are anyhow?!" Bedlington replies, "America, of course."

Kicked off the bus, Bedlington hitches a ride with an elderly black man in a horse-drawn cart (which later passes the broken down bus on the side of the road). This establishes the pattern of the book: railroad porters, baggage handlers, cleaning women, and lowly GIs are on Bedlington's side; senators, generals, and those in power give him a hard time. Bedlington becomes the subject of a tug-of-war, a culture war, over the meaning of America. *It Shouldn't Happen* must properly be seen as a contribution to the "Double V" campaign launched by the African American press in 1942: "The first V for victory over our enemies from without, the second V for victory over our enemies from within." In case the lesson is lost on the reader, when a police officer approaches Bedlington for reading offensive material on a park bench, the dog reveals the title: "Speeches by Lincoln."

Don Freeman's satire refuses to paint the army as a despoiled and corrupt institution that destroys those who serve in it. In fact, quite the opposite, the army is Bedlington's proper home, and he's eager to get back to camp—as dog or man—to rejoin his division, to do his duty, and to fight fascists overseas. We know Bedlington has internalized Frank Capra's "Why We Fight" series because he gives a rousing speech to his fellow dogs in the K-9 Corps so they will attack the Nazi dummies more ferociously. The main obstacle Bedlington faces in fulfilling his democratic destiny is a grandstanding and bloviating senator who, lacking any real work, drums up a phony scandal over Bedlington receiving an upper berth in a Pullman car. The senator--who bears a resemblance to any number of southern segregationist politicians, from James K. Vardaman to Theodore Bilbo—tracks Bedlington back to camp, where the dog delivers a well-deserved chomp to the demagogue's rear-end.

The book's penultimate twist is a telling one. The officer in charge of the K-9 Corps christens Bedlington "a real fighting man" for his attack on a homegrown fascist. That breaks the spell and turns Bedlington back into a man, who then boards ship to finish off the Axis.

Continued next week

When Harcourt Brace released *It Shouldn't Happen* on July 19, 1945, the war was over in Europe and nearly so in the Pacific. The first V achieved, the broad coalition that had pushed for civil rights since the 1930s focused on the second V, the enemies of democracy at home. During the war, well over a million African Americans had moved out of the Jim Crow South to the North and West in pursuit of defense jobs. Their fight against discrimination in the workplace and housing market, as well as in schools, public facilities, interstate commerce, and the military, was now taken up by the labor unions in the Congress of Industrial Organizations (CIO), A. Philip Randolph's Brotherhood of Sleeping Car Porters, the NAACP, the Communist Party (the only political party at the time to endorse racial equality), and progressive New Dealers. *It Shouldn't Happen* was one of the first postwar efforts of the cultural front to support this new Civil Rights initiative.

Few expected the backlash to be so ferocious, although it was foreshadowed by the anonymous *New York Times* review of *It Shouldn't Happen*. Within months of World War II's end, the right wing of the Democratic Party renewed its opposition to desegregation. The Ku Klux Klan enjoyed a resurgence in the South. Northern business proved cool to any talk of federal restrictions on their operations. And, most damaging, a broad anti-communism seized the nation's political agenda in response to the United States' erstwhile ally, the Soviet Union, acting as a hostile occupation force in conquered German territories. In March 1947, President Harry S. Truman declared the "Truman Doctrine" in a speech to Congress, launching the Cold War, and also initiated the federal loyalty-security program, which unleashed the Red Scare that would become known as "McCarthyism." Although the United States Armed Forces were desegregated by executive order in 1948, the purges, black lists, and un-American activities committees that followed put an end to the cultural front and the Depression-born social movement that had championed Civil Rights.

Cold War America of the 1950s, with its Baby Boom and Levittowns, its mass consumerism and upward mobility, had to find new ways to accommodate the demands for racial equality. In place of the labor-based insurgency of the 1930s and 1940s there arose a religious and youth-based movement centered on new activists like Martin Luther King, Jr., and new organizations like the Southern

Christian Leadership Conference and the Student Nonviolent Coordinating Committee.

Meanwhile, the artists, writers, and musicians associated with the cultural front either had to mute their political messages or suffer the black list. Don Freeman, resilient and optimistic as ever, turned to the growing market in children's books. He would eventually write and illustrate over twenty of them, gaining fame especially for *Corduroy,* his tender 1968 story that featured the first African-American heroine in children's trade literature. In the book, the heroine Lisa defies mainstream consumerist values to buy and care for a damaged department store teddy bear. Perhaps it's too much to see Corduroy-the-bear as an echo of Bedlington-the-dog, each deemed unworthy of upper-berths and department store shelves. But one can easily imagine young Lisa, after sewing on the bear's missing button in her tenement bedroom, as heading out into the world of the late 1960s, fulfilling her destiny, and championing the cause of equality.

TODD DePASTINO
February, 2014

IT SHOULDN'T HAPPEN
(TO A DOG)

what happened to

PVT. ALBERT C. BEDLINGTON JR.

Al was no different from any of the other fellows in our
barracks—at first.

There's no doubt he TRIED as hard as any guy could, but Army life didn't come easy to him.

Just when he started to change nobody can say. Maybe
it happened the day the lieutenant made him show his
dog tags—the way he looked at him.

Or perhaps it was that sergeant—

the way he'd yell at him—"C'mon, Bedlington, *crawl!*"

It seemed to Bedlington as if he were always on all fours.

As I say, no telling just how or when it happened. One night he was sitting on his top bunk, brooding. He brooded on into the night, and the following morning when he went in to shave, Bedlington had the shock of his life.

. . . What he'd been fearing for months had happened.

Terrified, he ran back to his bunk.

Then he reported on the sick list. Nobody noticed him.
Everybody was sick as a dog.

The Medics were frustrated,

so he was sent to the head psychiatrist, who found nothing unusual about his case and ordered him to return to duty.

Back in the barracks Al wondered what they would say about him.

He needn't have worried. When the fellas came in they all recognized him.

And so life went on as usual.

"Prepare for gas!"

"Say, Sergeant, which one is Bedlington?"

A
Three day
Pass

Al received a three-day pass from his commanding officer.

This was his first bus trip to town. He had never been out of camp before.

When he got on the bus it was already full of GIs.

"Hey, you! You can't sit there! Move on to the back seat. Where d'ya think y'are anyhow?!"

"America, of course," Al answered.

"You an' me better settle this outside."

That night
at the
USO

"Get this straight, Al, anywheres I can go, you can go too!"

"Good evening, boys."

"What did I tell ya? We all look alike to them."

It looked so easy to Al,

he had to try it.

This wasn't for him.

He decided he must be the intellectual type.

Next day, at the library.

He went to the park to read in peace.

THE
PARADE

"Major, get rid of those damn mutts out on the field!"

The major knew just the man for the job.

"Scram, you guys . . .

. . . we're having a big review today!"

"PASS IN REVIEW!"—

"You'll be charged with impersonating an officer!"
the MP told him.

THE
DECISION

Something had to be done.

"I have decided to send Bedlington on a furlough—but without a return trip ticket."

The order was posted.

"Hot dog!"

That night the gang had a send-off party for him at the camp PX.

Sergeant McGary gave a toast. "If you ever get in a jam in New York, just tell 'em you're a pal of McGary's. They all know me—I was on the police force once meself."

THE
FURLOUGH TRAIN

There didn't seem to be a seat.

He went to the baggage car.

While the train stopped for water . . .

"He's dead tired. Find him a decent place to sleep. He deserves the best!"

Surprisingly enough there was one upper berth vacant.

The next morning . . .

"How in hell did he get up there?"

"But he has his furlough papers with him," the porter explained.

During all the commotion Bedlington had disappeared.

Back in the baggage car the old baggage man said, "I was beginning to worry about you. We're nearly there."

Arrival
in
New York

In the heart of Times Square.

The news was already out.

MEANWHILE
IN
WASHINGTON D.C.

A Senator snoozed while one of his political opponents
was speaking, urging the passage of an important bill.

"Mister Speaker! I must interrupt. My attention has been called to a most disgraceful incident."

"Who said *who* don't know there's a war on?"

BACK IN NEW YORK

He sighted a civilian chow line,

and discovered he, too, was getting mighty hungry.

The civilians must be in a *bad* fix.

Bedlington nearly fainted from hunger on the way.

Inside . . . Standing Room Only.

The people comment.

YOU ASK ME-
SO I'M TELLING
YOU — I THINK
THE COUNTRY'S
GOIN' TO THE
DOGS

Then came the beauty contest.

He wanted to get away from it all,

but the hunger still persisted.

Ah, gum!

Nothing.

"Have you anything to say for yourself?"

There *must* be something . . .

"Sergeant McGary!"

They took Al across the street to Spike's Grill and gave
him a big feed.

Then they sent him to a first class hotel

where he spent the night.

HOME

Early the next morning something compelled him to
go . . .

. . . if only just to have a look . . .

Mother!

BACK TO CAMP

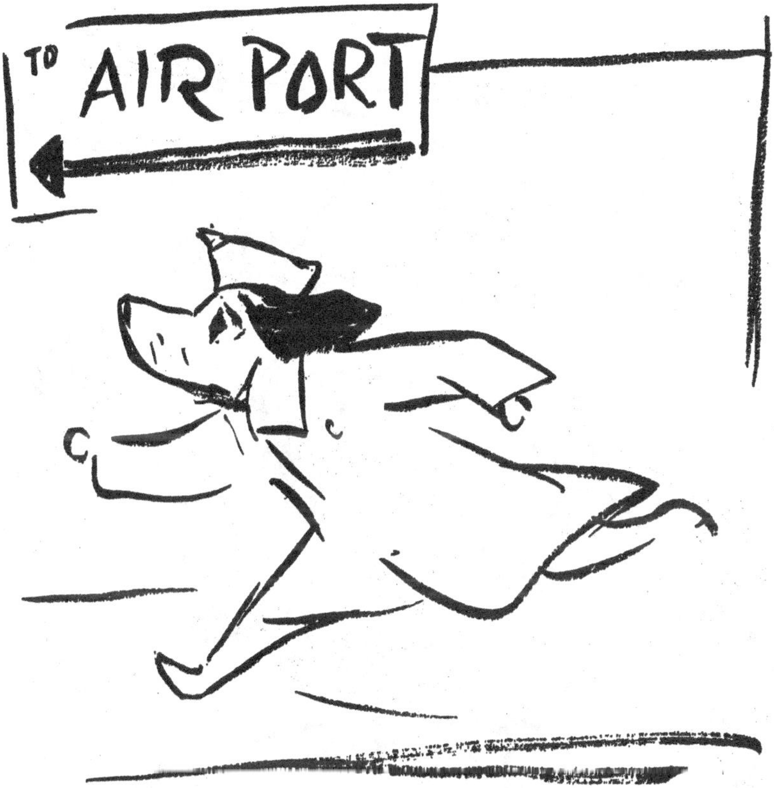
TO AIR PORT

"There's my camp!"

"They're moving out!"

"They didn't *expect* me to come back! . . . .

. . . Maybe some of the outfit is still here."

A note?

NEWS ITEM —
DOGS ARE NEEDED IN THE WAR EFFORT
We are going on maneuvers good luck Al,
the gang

"I bet next they'll be going overseas . . . without me."

JOINING UP

"You're accepted, Bedlington . . . but remember, on all fours now, no foolishness."

"Well, fellas, I'm in!"

The trainers were having a hard time making the dogs get mad.

Bedlington wondered why Butch didn't catch on.

He decided to show him.

"Say, have I got a smart new recruit!"

"Don't you realize what we're fighting for? If the trainers won't tell you, I will."

ENTER –
THE SENATOR

Hot on the trail.

"Do you mean to say you don't know about this scandal?"

"It's our Bedlington!"

"By golly, I'll get him yet—"

Could it be?

"Good! That Bedlington must be a real fighting man!"

"Does he mean me?"

"O.K., Bedlington—you made it!"